最高人民检察院
工作报告

WORK REPORT OF
THE SUPREME PEOPLE'S PROCURATORATE

2024

中国检察出版社

图书在版编目（CIP）数据

最高人民检察院工作报告 . 2024 : 汉文、英文 / 最高人民检察院编著 . -- 北京 : 中国检察出版社 , 2025. ISBN 978-7-5102-3230-5

Ⅰ . D926.31

中国国家版本馆 CIP 数据核字第 20253EE706 号

最高人民检察院工作报告 . 2024

Zuigao Renmin Jianchayuan Gongzuo Baogao.2024

最高人民检察院　编著

责任编辑：傅哲明
技术编辑：王英英
封面设计：徐嘉武

出版发行：中国检察出版社
社　　址：北京市石景山区香山南路 109 号（100144）
网　　址：中国检察出版社（www.zgjccbs.com）
编辑电话：（010）86423798
发行电话：（010）86423726　86423727　86423728
（010）86423730　68650016
经　　销：新华书店
印　　刷：北京联合互通彩色印刷有限公司
开　　本：787 mm × 1092 mm　16 开
印　　张：6.25
字　　数：50 千字
版　　次：2025 年 3 月第一版　　2025 年 3 月第一次印刷
书　　号：ISBN 978-7-5102-3230-5
定　　价：36.00 元

目　录

最高人民检察院工作报告

——2024年3月8日

在第十四届全国人民代表大会第二次会议上

最高人民检察院检察长　应　勇

各位代表：

现在，我代表最高人民检察院，向大会报告工作，请予审议，并请全国政协各位委员提出意见。

2023年工作回顾

2023年，在以习近平同志为核心的党中央坚强领导下，在全国人大及其常委会有力监督下，最高人民检察院坚持以习近平新时代中国特色社会主义思想为指导，全面贯彻党的二十大和二十届二中全会精神，认真落实十四届全国人大一次会议决议，深刻领悟“两个确立”的决定性意义，增强“四个意识”、坚定“四个自信”、做到“两个维护”，主动融入和服务中国式现代化，忠实履行宪法法律赋予的法律监督职责，高质效办好每一个案件，自觉为大局服务、为人民司法、为法治担当，扎实推进习近平法治思想的检察实践，各项检察工作取得新进展。全国检察机关共办理各类案件 425.3 万件，同比上升 28.9%。

一、为大局服务，充分履行检察职能维护稳定促进发展

紧紧围绕新时代新征程党和国家的中心任务，贯彻总体国家安全观，尊重和保障人权，切实履行法律监督职责，更好服务高质量发展和高水平安全。

坚决维护国家安全和社会稳定。依法惩治犯罪是检察机关维护稳定的基本职责。全年批准逮捕各类犯罪嫌疑人 72.6 万人，提起公诉 168.8 万人，同比分别上升 47.1% 和 17.3%。对严重犯罪保持“严”的震慑。依法严厉打击敌对势力渗透、破坏、颠覆、分裂活动。把开展反恐怖反分裂斗争

与推动维稳工作法治化常态化结合起来，促进新疆等地长治久安。深入推进常态化扫黑除恶斗争，起诉 1.5 万人。依法从严惩治故意杀人、抢劫、绑架等严重暴力犯罪，起诉 6.1 万人。突出惩治群众反映强烈的盗窃、诈骗、毒品犯罪，起诉 35 万人。配合公安机关开展命案积案攻坚，最高人民检察院对蒋四兴、薛三元锤杀船员等 137 起发案二十年以上的命案依法核准追诉，让正义虽久必至、虽远必达。

宽严相济促犯罪治理。全面准确落实宽严相济刑事政策，该严则严、当宽则宽、罚当其罪。对涉嫌犯罪但无逮捕必要的，决定不批捕 26.6 万人；对犯罪情节轻微，依法不需要判处刑罚或者免除刑罚的，决定不起诉 49.8 万人，同比分别上升 22.5% 和 12.6%。会同公安部制定羁押必要性审查工作规定，对不需要继续羁押的犯罪嫌疑人，依法变更强制措施 2.9 万人。依法适用认罪认罚从宽制度，超过 90% 的犯罪嫌疑人在检察环节认罪认罚，一审服判率 96.8%，高出未适用该制度案件 36 个百分点。会同最高人民法院、公安部、司法部制定专门意见，统一全国醉驾执法司法标准，形成行政处罚与刑事追究衔接的醉驾治理体系。

充分履行反腐败检察职责。受理各级监委移送职务犯罪 2 万人，同比上升 9.3%；已起诉 1.8 万人，其中原省部级干部25人。加强配合与制约，与国家监委共同规范提前介入工作，检察机关提前介入案件占受理案件的61.1%；自行补充侦查3020件、退回补充调查808件。积极参与行业性、系统性腐败治理，分别起诉金融、医疗领域职务犯罪348人和580人；指导湖北检察机关办理足球领域系列腐败案，已起诉中国足协原主席陈戌源等15人。落实受贿行贿一起查，起诉行贿犯罪2593人，同比上升18.9%。协同追逃追赃，对14名逃匿、死亡贪污贿赂犯罪嫌疑人向法院提出没收违法所得申请。中国银行开平支行原行长许国俊贪污挪用巨额公款后潜逃国外二十年，经持续追逃被强制遣返，广东检察机关依法起诉后其被判处无期徒刑，彰显有逃必追的坚定决心。

着力营造法治化营商环境。法治是最好的营商环境。注重运用法治方式稳定社会预期、提振市场信心，起诉破坏市场经济秩序犯罪12.1万人，同比上升20.4%。起诉虚开增值税专用发票、骗取出口退税等危害税收征管犯罪9428人，同比上升10.9%。对各类经营主体一视同仁对待，依法平等保护。制定推动民营经济发展壮大检察意见，严格区分经济纠纷与经济犯罪、行政违法与刑事犯罪、单位犯罪与个人犯罪等界限，持续清理涉企“挂案”，坚决纠正以刑事手段插手民事、经济纠纷，坚决纠正超范围超时限查封扣押冻结财产，促进优化民营经济发展环境。针对民营企业关键岗位人员职务侵占、挪用资金、受贿等侵害企业利益问题，出台 12 条检察举措，促进健全民营企业内部反腐机制，依法保护企业产权和企业家权益。

保障创新驱动发展。出台检察机关办理知识产权案件 45 条举措，强化综合保护。起诉侵犯商标权、专利权、著作权和商业秘密等犯罪 1.8 万人，同比上升 40.8%。加强诉讼环节商业秘密保护，防止“二次泄密”。办理知识产权民事行政诉讼监督案件 2508 件，是 2022 年的 2.7 倍。办理知识产权领域公益诉讼 873 件。开展涉知识产权恶意诉讼专项监督。某文化传媒公司假冒音乐电视作品著作权人提起恶意诉讼 5800 余件，最高人民检察院挂牌督办，指导广东、山东等 9 个省市检察机关同步依法监督法院再审，并批准逮捕 5 名犯罪嫌疑人，促进营造良好创新生态。

坚决维护金融安全。制定服务保障金融高质量发展 23 条检察意见，严厉打击金融犯罪，防范化解金融风险。起诉金融诈骗、破坏金融管理秩序犯罪 2.7 万人，其中集资诈骗、非法吸收公众存款犯罪 1.8 万人，保持惩治涉众型金融犯罪高压态势，尽最大努力追赃挽损。协同完善证券犯罪执法司法标准，挂牌督办重大案件，起诉欺诈发行、内幕交易、操纵市场等证券犯罪346人，共同维护资本市场安全、维护中小投资者合法权益。会同国家外汇管理局发布典型案例，从严打击涉外汇违法犯罪。与各级监委、公安机关加强反洗钱协作，起诉洗钱犯罪2971人，同比上升14.9%。项某帮助他人掩饰、隐瞒犯罪所得，高价收购“虚拟币”并通过境外交易商抛售，非法汇兑18亿余元至境外，上海检察机关依法提起公诉，决不让“黑钱”漂“白”。

推动网络空间依法治理。制定检察机关网络法治工作21条意见，起诉利用网络实施的犯罪32.3万人，同比上升36.2%。坚决惩治网络暴力“按键伤人”，会同最高人民法院、公安部制定指导意见，对在网上肆意造谣诽谤、谩骂侮辱、“人肉搜索”等涉嫌犯罪的，依法提起公诉，追究刑事责任，维护公民人格权益和网络秩序。严厉打击“网络水军”造谣引流、舆情敲诈等违法犯罪，净化网络舆论环境。依法严惩电诈网赌，积极参与打击涉缅北电信网络诈骗专项行动，深挖严打组织者、领导者及幕后“金主”，起诉电信网络诈骗犯罪5.1万人、帮助信息网络犯罪14.7万人、网络赌博犯罪1.9万人，同比分别上升66.9%、13%和5.3%。针对互联网领域侵犯个人信息、虚假宣传、消费欺诈等乱象，办理公益诉讼6766件，督促落实监管责任和平台责任，用法治力量维护网络清朗。

推进社会治理。在履职办案中弘扬社会主义核心价值观，促进法治社会建设。持续引领正当防卫理念，审查认定属正当防卫依法不捕不诉261人，同比上升25.5%。快餐店老板与持刀闯入店内敲诈行凶的歹徒对砍致其死亡，棋牌室管理员制止酒后持刀滋事者将其划伤，检察机关均认定不构成犯罪，"法不能向不法让步"。坚持罪责刑相适应，在法律框架内寻求公平正义"最大公约数"。某学院副院长猥亵未成年女生，该生父亲愤而将其打成轻伤涉嫌犯罪，检察机关综合考量，对事出有因、情节较轻且自首的打人者依法决定不起诉；对仅被行政拘留的猥亵者监督立案，依法追究刑事责任，彰显法理情统一的司法力量。坚持标本兼治，结合履职办案发出检察建议3.9万份。最高人民检察院分别向国家粮食和物资储备局、中储粮集团公司发出第九号、十号检察建议，防治职务犯罪，共护粮食安全；针对养老机构内侵犯老年人人身权利问题，向民政部发出第十一号检察建议，促进强化监管。北京检察机关深挖办案中发现的涉及上万张特种作业假操作证问题，推动查办制贩假证人员126人，督促主管部门落实监管责任，溯源整治假冒国家机关官方网站226个。

服务乡村全面振兴。专题部署服务“三农”工作。着力维护农村社会和谐稳定，起诉农村宗族黑恶势力犯罪604人。依法惩治制售假冒伪劣农资犯罪，起诉820人；指导吉林、黑龙江、河南等地检察机关开展农机安全领域公益诉讼，维护农业生产安全。依法守护耕地红线、保护高标准农田，起诉非法占用农用地犯罪2883人，办理涉土地保护公益诉讼9753件。针对废弃农用薄膜散落田间造成污染，指导江西、贵州、青海、新疆等地检察机关以专项监督促进清理回收，保护土壤生态。向因案致生活陷入困境的1.3万名农村地区受害人发放司法救助金1.1亿元。

加强历史文化遗产司法保护。协同开展打击防范文物犯罪专项工作，起诉盗掘古墓葬、倒卖文物等犯罪2089人，同比上升37.4%。办理历史文化遗产保护领域公益诉讼2734件。会同国家文物局发布惩治文物犯罪、长城保护公益诉讼典型案例。与住房城乡建设部加强协作，推动城乡历史文化保护传承。指导辽宁、江西、广西、重庆等地检察机关加强红色资源公益保护，山西、福建、海南、西藏、青海等地检察机关加强石窟寺文物、涉台文物、南海文物、传统村落和非物质文化遗产公益保护，用法治守护中华文脉。

服务区域协调发展。深化区域检察协作，更好服务西部大开发、东北全面振兴、中部地区加快崛起、东部地区加快推进现代化。指导京津冀检察机关优化协作举措，共促法治化营商环境建设和区域生态环境治理，服务高标准高质量建设雄安新区。指导沪苏浙皖检察机关完善跨区域一体履职机制。支持广东检察机关服务保障粤港澳大湾区建设。指导海南检察机关服务保障自贸港建设。制定专门意见，服务保障成渝地区双城经济圈、新时代壮美广西建设。

服务高水平对外开放。依法办理涉外刑事案件4243件、刑事司法协助案件220件，平等保护中外当事人合法权益，促进高质量共建“一带一路”走深走实。最高人民检察院开通英文官方网站，在陕西举办上海合作组织成员国总检察长会议，巩固深化中国—东盟成员国总检察长会议、金砖国家总检察长会议、国际检察官联合会等多边司法合作机制，发挥中国—东盟成员国检察官交流培训基地作用，讲好新时代中国法治故事，助力大国外交。

二、为人民司法，在检察履职中保障和改善民生

紧紧围绕落实以人民为中心的发展思想，牢固树立“如我在诉”的理念，“把屁股端端地坐在老百姓的这一面”，确保检察权为人民行使、让人民满意。

守护群众身边安全。积极参与安全生产风险专项整治，对重大安全生产事故案挂牌督办，起诉重大责任事故、危险作业等犯罪4750人，办理该领域公益诉讼1.7万件。黑龙江检察机关开展校园场馆安全公益诉讼专项监督，督促整治隐患5500余处。对制售有毒有害食品、假药劣药犯罪加大打击力度，坚决依法严惩，起诉1.3万人，同比上升31.5%。办理食药安全领域公益诉讼2.4万件，同比上升16.8%。协同开展道路交通安全专项整治，发出检察建议7442件，推动治理驾驶资格监管漏洞、违法限高限速等问题。与国家邮政局等持续推进平安寄递见成效，起诉寄递毒品、枪支弹药爆炸物犯罪3139人，同比下降36.3%。会同市场监管总局等专项治理医疗美容行业非法行医、制假售假、虚假宣传等问题。依法惩治故意伤医扰医犯罪，起诉226人，同比下降51.6%。协同整治医保领域欺诈骗保，依法守护老百姓的“救命钱”。

强化生态环境司法保护。协同整治危险废物污染环境、第三方环保服务机构弄虚作假，起诉污染环境犯罪3831人，同比下降11.3%。加大对破坏资源保护领域犯罪惩治力度，起诉3.5万人，同比上升6.4%。办理环境资源领域公益诉讼8.4万件。贯彻长江保护法，最高人民检察院直接对长江干支流船舶污染问题以公益诉讼立案，沿江检察机关同步办理关联案件 575 件，推动船舶污染物接收处置全闭环。贯彻黄河保护法，举办首届服务保障黄河国家战略检察论坛，会同水利部开展黄河流域水资源保护专项行动。协同国家林草局抓实林草湿荒保护治理。会同中国海警局等专项整治盗采海砂。指导河北、内蒙古、黑龙江、吉林等地检察机关专项监督外来物种治理、荒漠化防治、黑土地保护。向全国人大常委会专项报告环境资源检察工作，得到有力监督支持。

依法化解涉法涉诉矛盾纠纷。坚持和发展新时代“枫桥经验”，扎实推进检察信访工作法治化。部署信访矛盾源头治理三年攻坚行动，各级检察院领导干部包案办理信访案件 4.6 万件；排查交办 1062 件重复信访积案，已办结 1024 件。最高人民检察院和山东、宁夏等 7 个省区市检察机关会同司法行政机关开展试点，对申诉人首次提出刑事申诉、请求国家赔偿的，由公益律师免费代理。做实群众信访件件有回复，收到 88.6 万件信访，7 日内程序性回复率 99.8%，3 个月内办理过程或结果答复率 97.3%。

保护未成年人健康成长。对性侵、伤害、虐待等侵害未成年人犯罪“零容忍”，起诉 6.7 万人，同比上升 14.9%。对涉罪未成年人坚持教育、感化、挽救方针，情节较轻的，依法附条件不起诉 3.1 万人；犯罪严重的，依法起诉 3.9 万人。

强化未成年人犯罪预防，推进罪错未成年人分级干预，协调推动河北、广东、广西、贵州、云南等地加强专门学校建设，依法教育矫治有严重不良行为的未成年人。会同全国妇联等发布家庭教育指导典型案例，制发督促监护令5.7万份。与教育行政等部门联动，共建2120个青少年法治教育实践基地，建立涉案未成年人控辍保学协作机制。推动落实密切接触未成年人单位入职查询制度、侵害未成年人强制报告制度。发布未成年人网络保护指导性案例，严惩“隔空猥亵”、线上联系线下侵害等犯罪，协同防治网络沉迷，引导安全用网上网。推动主管部门完善电竞酒店、盲盒市场、剧本杀、密室逃脱等监管制度，促进破解新业态未成年人保护难题。优化检察综合履职，携手各方为孩子们撑起法治蓝天。

依法维护妇女合法权益。部署全面加强妇女权益司法保护。依法严惩侵犯妇女生命健康、人格尊严等犯罪，起诉4.6万人，同比上升10.7%。一犯罪嫌疑人将偷拍的女性露脸隐私视频发布在网上，江苏检察机关以侮辱罪提起公诉。起诉家庭暴力犯罪563人。与全国妇联开展专项工作，对遭受犯罪侵害或民事侵权，无法通过诉讼获得有效赔偿、生活面临急迫困难的2.3万名妇女予以司法救助。深化妇女权益保障公益诉讼，重点监督就业歧视、贬损妇女人格等违法行为，办理相关公益诉讼 1490 件。发布典型案例，依法保护农村妇女涉土地合法权益。与人力资源社会保障部、国家卫生健康委、全国总工会等出台规范指引，推动完善女职工特殊劳动保护、消除工作场所性骚扰制度。在四级检察院开设接待专窗，畅通妇女儿童权益特殊保护的“绿色通道”。

依法保护特定群体合法权益。会同民政部、住房城乡建设部、中国残联发布两批典型案例，依法保障残疾人就业、教育、康复等权益。办理无障碍环境建设领域公益诉讼 1983 件，让爱无“碍”，共享美好生活。针对药品说明书“字小如蚁”影响用药安全，指导江苏、上海等地检察机关以公益诉讼推动大字版、简化版等适老化改造；天津检察机关推动公交软件增加语音报站功能；湖北检察机关推动急救电话增加文字报警功能，保障老年人和残疾人便捷融入社会生活。积极参与欠薪治理，发布惩治恶意欠薪犯罪典型案例，起诉 1082 人，追索欠薪 3.8 亿元。对权益受损但因经济困难或法律知识欠缺，无力起诉的农民工、残疾人、老年人等，支持提起民事诉讼 7.7 万件，同比上升 16.8%，保障公民依法享有诉权、有效行使诉权。

坚决守护“国防绿”“英烈红”。依法惩治危害国防利益、侵犯军人军属和英雄烈士合法权益犯罪，起诉 364 人，同比上升7.1%。办理国防和军事领域、军人权益保护领域公益诉讼1202件。持续推进军用机场净空、军用港口和舰艇航道保护专项监督。协同加强部队训练场安全风险防控，防止非法挖捡买卖未爆弹药干扰战备训练、危害公共安全。协同开展“守护戎装”专项行动，依法惩治非法制售军服犯罪。救助遭受不法侵害的军人军属、退役军人1331名。办理英烈权益保护领域公益诉讼875件。针对一些散葬烈士墓管护不到位问题，山东检察机关携手退役军人事务部门持续三年开展专项活动，督促集中迁建或就地保护5326处。3名网络自媒体博主恶意制作、传播虚假视频，将一开国少将污蔑成叛徒，浙江军地检察协作，依法提起民事公益诉讼，责令公开赔礼道歉并承担公益损害赔偿责任，英烈荣光不容亵渎。

切实维护港澳台同胞、海外侨胞和归侨侨眷合法权益。依法办理涉港澳台和涉侨案件。深化与港澳司法机构、廉政公署高层交流和务实合作，为港澳司法法律界人士开设研修培训课程。携手中国侨联，指导省级检侨合作，护航侨企发展、维护侨胞权益。指导福建检察机关制定服务两岸融合发展示范区建设意见，为台胞台企提供优质法律服务。

三、为法治担当，以检察监督促进社会公平正义

紧紧围绕“努力让人民群众在每一个司法案件中感受到公平正义”的目标，让“高质效办好每一个案件”成为新时代新征程检察履职办案的基本价值追求，在实体上确保实现公平正义，在程序上让公平正义更好更快实现，在效果上让人民群众可感受、能感受、感受到公平正义。

深化刑事立案、侦查和审判监督。与公安部、国家安全部、海关总署、中国海警局完善侦查监督与协作配合机制。对侦查机关应当立案而不立案、不应当立案而立案的，监督立案、撤案 13.9 万件，同比上升 68.2%。对不构成犯罪或证据不足的，依法不批捕 21 万人、不起诉 5.4 万人，同比分别上升 51.1% 和 10.4%；对应当逮捕、应当起诉而未提请逮捕、未移送起诉的，追加逮捕 1.9 万人、追加起诉 9.9 万人，同比分别上升 12.8% 和 66%。对认为确有错误的刑事裁判提出抗诉 7876 件，法院已审结 6114 件，其中改判、发回重审 4885 件，改变率 79.9%。陈仓伙同他人入室盗窃，被发现后杀人灭口，案发十七年后被查获。因其翻供，原审法院认为证据间存在矛盾判其无罪，最高人民检察院审查认为现有证据已形成完整链条，能排除合理怀疑，依法提出抗诉，被改判为死缓。四川检察机关审查“毛某强奸杀人案”时，发现客观

证据不能认定其作案，真凶另有他人，督促公安机关依法释放并持续跟进监督，十四年后真凶落网。让有罪者受惩、还无辜者清白，彰显法治正义。

加强刑事执行监督。最高人民检察院组织制定巡回检察三年规划，直接对4所监狱、4个看守所开展巡回检察，在福建、河南、重庆、甘肃等9个省区市试点社区矫正巡回检察。会同最高人民法院、司法部等制定依法推进假释适用、规范暂予监外执行指导意见，既监督纠正“纸面服刑”“提钱出狱”，又防止该减不减、该放不放。受理减刑、假释、暂予监外执行监督案件同比上升25.2%；对提请、决定或裁定不当的，提出检察意见2.6万人次。对监外执行条件消失的，督促收监执行3652人。加强财产刑执行监督，提出纠正意见9.5万件，推动执行6.7亿元。

做优民事诉讼监督。对认为确有错误的民事裁判提出抗诉和再审检察建议1.4万件，法院已审结8537件，其中改判、发回重审、调解及和解撤诉7549件，改变率88.4%，最高人民检察院对41件典型案件提出抗诉。会同最高人民法院规范民事再审检察建议案件办理，加强同级监督。对民事审判和执行活动违法情形提出检察建议13万件。对5.5万件不支持监督申请案件强化释法说理，维护司法权威。开展虚假诉讼监督，依法纠正9359件，起诉虚假诉讼犯罪925人。某涉黑组织围猎司法工作人员，以虚假诉讼逃废债务，辽宁检察机关在依法惩治涉黑犯罪及其“保护伞”的同时，督促纠正相关案件184件。

加大行政诉讼监督力度。对认为确有错误的行政裁判提出抗诉和再审检察建议624件，法院已审结305件，其中改判、发回重审、调解及和解撤诉231件，改变率75.7%。对行政审判和执行活动违法情形提出检察建议4.5万件。会同有关部门实质性化解行政争议2.2万件，其中争议十年以上的780件。湖南某县两个村民小组因山林田土权属纷争，不接受行政决定、不执行行政判决，发生4次械斗致18人获刑。市县两级检察院受理监督申请后，会同当地政府引导村民从对抗走向对话，持续二十余年的争议终得化解。

推动检察监督与行政执法有机衔接。探索行政违法行为监督，对履行法律监督职责中发现的行政机关违法行使职权或者不行使职权行为，提出检察建议3.2万件，同比上升50.2%。深化强制隔离戒毒检察监督试点，提出检察建议2036件。推动行政执法与刑事司法双向衔接，督促行政执法机关移送涉嫌犯罪案件5869件，防止以罚代刑；对被不起诉人应受行政处罚的，提出检察意见，移送主管机关处理11.3

万人，防止当罚不罚。

深化公益诉讼检察。检察公益诉讼制度是习近平法治思想在公益保护领域的原创性成果。牢记“公共利益代表”神圣职责，立案办理公益诉讼19万件，其中行政公益诉讼16.8万件。向行政机关发出诉前检察建议11.6万件，回复整改率99.1%，绝大多数公益损害问题在诉前得到解决。对发出公告或检察建议后仍未解决的，依法提起诉讼1.3万件，99.96%得到裁判支持。完善代表建议、政协提案与检察公益诉讼衔接转化机制，与中央统战部和各民主党派中央共建“益心为公”志愿者检察云平台。有志愿者反映网购的灭火器无法灭火，安徽检察机关调查发现该类灭火器确有重大安全隐患，遂以检察建议督促主管部门专项整治、强化监管，查获伪劣灭火器数百万具，抓获涉案人员22人。全国人大常委会已将制定检察公益诉讼法列入立法计划，最高人民检察院积极配合，推动公益司法保护的“中国方案”法制化。

加大检察侦查工作力度。检察侦查是法律赋予检察机关的重要职能。对在诉讼监督中发现的司法工作人员利用职权实施的徇私枉法、滥用职权、刑讯逼供等犯罪，依法立案侦查1976人，同比上升36.5%。十年前4名监狱民警殴打一服刑人员致死，编造系因病死亡，其家属多年控告未果。最高人民检察院巡回检察中发现该线索并交办，甘肃检察机关立案侦查，4 人均被判处有期徒刑。对公安机关管辖的国家机关工作人员利用职权实施的重大犯罪案件，确需检察机关直接受理的，依法立案侦查 176 人。某派出所副所长伙同他人组局敲诈，湖南检察机关立案查办 8 人，依法追究刑事责任。司法腐败严重损害司法公正、影响司法公信，必须依法严惩。

数字检察赋能法律监督。制定数字检察规划，构建“业务主导、数据整合、技术支撑、重在应用”的工作机制。天津检察机关研发骗税类案监督模型，筛查出假报货物名称、虚增产品数量、虚假收汇结汇等异常数据上万条，移送相关部门查处，并以检察建议督促行政机关堵塞漏洞、强化监管、挽回损失。北京、山西、浙江、四川等地检察机关研发公租房违规使用、临时用地到期未复垦、中介机构出具虚假检测报告、违法抽取城市地下水等法律监督大数据应用模型，促进系统治理，维护公共利益。

四、接受人民监督，确保检察权依法正确行使

监督者更要接受监督，在人民监督下依法履职。

自觉接受人大监督。深入学习贯彻十四届全国人大一次会议精神，组织四级检察院一体落实。聘请 95 名全国人大代

表担任新一届特约监督员。邀请全国人大代表视察检察工作、参与检察活动1715人次；走访2239名全国人大代表，当面听取意见。认真研究全国人大代表审议报告、调研座谈时提出的3016条意见建议，逐条落实、逐人回复。认真办理全国人大代表提出的230件书面建议，转化为改进工作的务实举措。内蒙古、江苏、安徽、贵州、陕西等省级人大常委会专门就加强法律监督、检察建议工作作出决定，有力保障检察机关依法履职。

自觉接受民主监督。邀请全国政协委员参与专题调研、公开听证等活动296人次。认真办理全国政协委员提出的72件提案。组织特约检察员专题调研公益诉讼检察工作。加强与各民主党派、工商联和无党派人士常态化联系，通报工作情况，听取意见建议。深化与全国工商联协作，共同举办民营经济法治建设峰会、民营企业家专场检察开放日活动，共促民营经济健康发展。

自觉接受履职制约。对公安机关提请复议复核的不捕不诉案件依法全面审查。对法院宣告无罪的公诉案件逐案复查、落实责任。分别与最高人民法院、司法部建立年度交流会商机制。与最高人民法院、司法部、全国律协建立年度四方会商机制。与司法部、全国律协制定保障律师执业权利十条意见并联合督导落实，纠正执法司法人员侵犯律师执业权利 2355 件，同比上升 32.3%。

自觉接受社会监督。向案件当事人全面公开办案进程、处理结果，向社会及时公开重要案件办理情况、检察法律文书，每季度发布检察办案数据、典型类案等。做实检察公开听证，对有争议有影响的审查逮捕、拟不起诉、信访申诉等案件，邀请人大代表、政协委员、专家学者等参与评议，帮助当事人解“法结”、化“心结”。共举行听证 25.8 万件次，同比上升 22.1%，其中信访案件听证后化解率 78.6%。常态化开展检察开放日活动。人民监督员监督检察办案 24.8 万件次，同比上升 96.1%。对媒体反映的涉检问题快速核查、及时回应，真诚接受监督。让检察权在阳光下运行，以公开促公正赢公信。

五、强化自身建设，锻造新时代检察铁军

落实全面从严治党要求，制定实施新时代检察队伍建设意见，锤炼忠诚干净担当的检察队伍。

深入开展主题教育。牢牢把握“学思想、强党性、重实践、建新功”总要求，深入学思践悟习近平新时代中国特色社会主义思想，让坚定拥护“两个确立”、坚决做到“两

个维护”成为新时代新征程检察机关的鲜明政治底色。持续加强政治建设，制定政治素质考察办法，组织政治轮训，不断提高政治判断力、政治领悟力、政治执行力。加强检察文化建设，弘扬检察英模精神，表彰38个全国模范检察院和马玮玮、屈欣等59名全国模范检察官，培育“忠诚、为民、担当、公正、廉洁”的新时代检察精神，让求真务实、担当实干成为检察人员的鲜明履职特征。

加强专业素能建设。制定检察教育培训五年规划，常态化开展检察官与其他执法司法人员、律师同堂培训。评选49名全国检察业务专家，举办全国十佳公诉人等业务竞赛，培养检察业务领军人才。制定司法解释和司法解释性质文件28件，发布指导性案例33件。深化检校合作，邀请11名专家学者到最高人民检察院挂职，组织106名检察实务专家进校园，精选180门检察实务课程进课堂，共建38家检察研究基地，推动习近平法治思想理论研究与实践应用相融互促。

强化检察业务管理。制定加快推进新时代检察业务管理现代化的意见，健全检察业务指导体系、评价体系、制约监督体系，遵循司法规律，引导树立正确政绩观，把“有质量的数量”和“有数量的质量”统筹在更加注重质量上。与2022年相比，个案平均审查起诉时间减少4.8天，捕后判决无罪和免予刑事处罚下降 24.8%，受理刑事赔偿案件下降 30.5%，抗诉案件改变率上升 6.3 个百分点，不服检察机关处理决定的信访下降 7.9%，法律监督工作质效明显提升。

深化司法体制综合配套改革。制定检察改革五年规划，明确 36 项改革任务。完善一体履职机制，在全国人大常委会法工委支持下，规范上级检察院统一调用辖区检察人员办案制度。深化检察人员分类管理，完善检察官遴选制度，优化检察官助理培养。四级院检察长常态化列席同级法院审委会会议。推动天津、云南、宁夏、新疆等 15 个省区市建立党委政法委执法监督与检察机关法律监督衔接机制。

全面准确落实司法责任制。坚持放权与管权并重、管案与管人结合，坚持突出检察官办案主体地位与检察长领导检察院工作相统一，检察长切实负起“管”检察官办案的责任。完善检察官惩戒、权益保障制度。围绕刑事案件不捕不诉、民事案件抗诉等重点环节，进一步健全内外部、上下级制约监督机制。开展执法司法突出问题专项检查，纠治检察履职存在的问题，促进检察权依法公正高效廉洁运行。加强对最高人民检察院自办案件监督管理，专项清理未结积案，以上率下规范履职。

深化全面从严治检。法律监督机关要敢于监督、善于监督，更要勇于自我监督。坚持严的基调，深化干部队伍教育整顿，坚决防治“灯下黑”。扛起系统内巡视政治责任，制定五年规划，扎实开展对省级检察院党组第一轮巡视。剖析通报检察人员违纪违法典型案件，以身边人身边事做实警示教育。持续深化落实防止干预司法“三个规定”，有问必记录，逢案必倒查，有责必追究，检察人员记录报告 23.8 万件，同比上升 40.8%。坚决支持纪检监察机关监督执纪问责，最高人民检察院 3 人因违纪违法被查处；地方检察机关 413 人因利用检察权违纪违法被查处，同比下降 13.1%，其中追究刑事责任 78 人，同比下降 20.4%。

着力夯实基层基础。牢固树立大抓基层鲜明导向，深化上级检察院领导干部联系基层机制，协助地方党委配齐配强基层院领导班子。加大培训力度，最高人民检察院直接培训基层检察人员 2.1 万人，其中基层院检察长 685 名。会同财政部制定基层院装备配备标准。深化检察对口援助，组织讲师团到西部地区巡讲支教，选派 322 名业务骨干到西藏、新疆、青海支援工作。优选 20 名基层院检察长到最高人民检察院挂职，选派最高人民检察院 28 名优秀年轻干部到基层一线“墩苗”。

各位代表，迈上新征程，伴随党和国家各项事业取得新的重大成就，人民检察事业稳步前进。这根本在于习近平总书记领航掌舵，在于习近平新时代中国特色社会主义思想科学指引，也是全国人大及其常委会有力监督、国务院大力支持、全国政协民主监督，国家监察委员会、最高人民法院配合与制约，各民主党派、工商联和无党派人士、各人民团体热忱关心，地方各级党政机关、各位代表、各位委员和社会各界支持帮助的结果。我谨代表最高人民检察院表示衷心感谢！

我们清醒认识到，检察工作还有不少突出问题。一是运用习近平法治思想指导检察履职仍需加强，融入国家治理、服务高质量发展的深度不够，检察为民还需进一步做实。二是法律监督职责履行存在薄弱环节，不敢监督、不善监督、监督不力的问题仍然存在，行政检察、民事检察仍是短板弱项。三是检察人员监督办案理念、素质能力不适应人民群众对公平正义的更高要求，队伍专业化水平有待提升。四是一些检察政策、措施在基层落实不够，基层基础工作仍待加强。五是司法体制综合配套改革仍需深化，检察权运行制约监督机制尚待完善，司法不公、司法腐败问题仍有发生。我们将采取有力措施，努力加以解决。

2024 年工作安排

2024 年，全国检察机关要坚持以习近平新时代中国特色社会主义思想为指导，全面贯彻党的二十大和二十届二中全会精神，坚定拥护“两个确立”、坚决做到“两个维护”，深入落实《中共中央关于加强新时代检察机关法律监督工作的意见》，从政治上着眼，从法治上着力，高质效办好每一个案件，保障国家法律统一正确实施，持续推进习近平法治思想的检察实践，以检察工作现代化支撑和服务中国式现代化。

第一，始终坚持党对检察工作的绝对领导。自觉融入党和国家工作大局，坚持党的中心工作推动到哪里，检察工作就跟进到哪里。强化检察机关党的政治建设，巩固拓展主题教育成果，健全检察机关学习贯彻党的创新理论制度机制，持续推动以学铸魂、以学增智、以学正风、以学促干。推进党建与业务深度融合，抓党建带队建促业务。

第二，坚决维护国家安全、社会安定、人民安宁。全力投入更高水平的平安中国建设，依法严惩危害国家安全犯罪、严重暴力犯罪、重大毒品犯罪和严重经济犯罪，不断增强人民群众安全感。依法推进常态化扫黑除恶斗争，打早打小、打准打实，不降格、不拔高。完善监检衔接机制，推进反腐败斗争。协同开展“净网”行动，专项打击整治网络谣言，依法惩治网络犯罪，促进依法管网治网。深入打击整治电信网络诈骗犯罪。充分发挥检察建议作用，促进社会治理。落实“谁执法谁普法”的普法责任制，结合办案强化法治宣传教育，助力加快建设法治社会。深化军地检察协作，服务推进新兴领域战略能力建设，有力维护国防利益和军人军属、英雄烈士、军队文职人员、退役军人合法权益。加强涉外检察工作，深化检察国际交流合作，坚决捍卫国家主权、安全、发展利益。

第三，依法服务高质量发展这个新时代的硬道理。完整准确全面贯彻新发展理念，与宏观政策取向保持一致，坚持稳中求进、以进促稳、先立后破，为我国经济回升向好、长期向好提供法治保障。开展“检察护企”专项行动，加强涉企经济犯罪案件的立案监督和侦查活动监督，加强涉企民事行政案件检察监督，推动持续优化法治化营商环境，用法治增强企业发展信心。从严惩治金融犯罪，服务金融高质量发展。强化反垄断和反不正当竞争司法，促进建设全国统一大市场。加强关键核心技术、新兴产业领域知识产权司法保护，服务数字经济建设，推动新质生产力加快发展。加强环境资源检察工作，守护蓝天碧水净土。助力文化事业和文化产业繁荣发展，服务文化强国建设。融入平安、法治、美丽乡村建设，服务乡村全面振兴。

第四，高质效履行法律监督职责。坚持依法一体履职、综合履职，推动刑事、民事、行政、公益诉讼“四大检察”全面协调充分发展。全面加强对立案、侦查、审判、执行等诉讼活动的法律监督，坚决防止和纠正冤错案件，维护司法公正。着力推动构建以证据为中心的刑事指控体系。推动审查起诉阶段律师辩护全覆盖。依法保障律师执业权利。深化“派驻＋巡回”检察机制，加强对刑罚执行和监管活动的监督。开展民事虚假诉讼专项监督。稳步推进行政违法行为监督。以专门立法为契机，进一步加强公益诉讼检察工作。深入实施数字检察战略。深化党委政法委执法监督与检察机关法律监督衔接机制，探索建立法律监督与法治督察衔接配合机制，让法律监督更有力有效。

第五，做实人民群众能体验得实惠的检察为民。践行司法为民宗旨，开展“检护民生”专项行动。深入推进检察信访工作法治化，持续加强信访矛盾源头治理和积案化解，加大支持起诉、司法救助力度，深化检察听证，打造新时代“枫桥经验”检察版。坚决从严惩治危害安全生产犯罪，加强食药安全、医保、个人信息保护等民生领域司法保障。与相关部门深化协作，依法保护未成年人、老年人、妇女、残疾人、农民工合法权益，合力保障灵活就业和新就业形态劳动者权益。

第六，持之以恒提升法律监督能力。深入贯彻习近平总书记关于党的自我革命的重要思想，坚持全面从严治检，一体加强政治能力、业务素能和职业道德建设。深化人才强检，加强知识产权、金融证券、涉外法治等紧缺人才培养。深化落实检察改革规划，强化检察权运行制约监督，修订完善落实司法责任制意见、司法责任追究条例，落实检察官惩戒制度，强化检察业务管理，优化检务公开，进一步加强基层基础建设。深入学习贯彻新修订的纪律处分条例，扎实开展集中性纪律教育，以自身净确保自身硬，建设过硬检察队伍。

各位代表，新时代新征程，我们将更加紧密团结在以习近平同志为核心的党中央周围，全面落实本次会议要求，更加自觉接受人大监督、民主监督和社会监督，依法履行法律监督职责，奋力开创人民检察事业新局面，努力为以中国式现代化全面推进强国建设、民族复兴伟业作出更大贡献！

附件

有关用语说明

1 羁押必要性审查

刑事诉讼法第九十五条规定，犯罪嫌疑人、被告人被逮捕后，人民检察院仍应当对羁押的必要性进行审查。审查认为犯罪嫌疑人、被告人不需要继续羁押的，应当建议公安机关、人民法院予以释放或者变更强制措施。对于审查起诉阶段的案件，应当及时决定释放或者变更强制措施。2023年11月，最高人民检察院、公安部联合印发《人民检察院公安机关羁押必要性审查、评估工作规定》，进一步规范羁押强制措施适用，依法保障犯罪嫌疑人、被告人合法权益。

2 没收违法所得申请

刑事诉讼法第二百九十八条、第三百条规定，对于贪污贿赂犯罪、恐怖活动犯罪等重大犯罪案件，犯罪嫌疑人、被告人逃匿，在通缉一年后不能到案，或者犯罪嫌疑人、被告人死亡，依照刑法规定应当追缴其违法所得及其他涉案财产的，人民检察院可以向人民法院提出没收违法所得的申请。人民法院经审理，对经查证属于违法所得及其他涉案财产，除依法返还被害人的以外，应当裁定予以没收。

❸ 行政违法行为监督

2014 年 10 月，党的十八届四中全会通过的《中共中央关于全面推进依法治国若干重大问题的决定》明确提出，检察机关在履行职责中发现行政机关违法行使职权或者不行使职权的行为，应该督促其纠正。2021 年 6 月，《中共中央关于加强新时代检察机关法律监督工作的意见》进一步明确，检察机关在履行法律监督职责中发现行政机关违法行使职权或者不行使职权的，可以依照法律规定制发检察建议等督促其纠正。

❹ 检察公益诉讼法

2014 年 10 月，党的十八届四中全会部署“探索建立检察机关提起公益诉讼制度”。2015年7月，全国人大常委会授权最高人民检察院在13个省区市检察机关开展试点。2017年6月，全国人大常委会修改民事诉讼法、行政诉讼法，正式建立检察公益诉讼制度。2019年10月，党的十九届四中全会要求“拓展公益诉讼案件范围”。全国人大常委会在制定、修订相关法律时陆续增加检察公益诉讼条款。2022年10月，党的二十大报告专门部署“完善公益诉讼制度”。十四届全国人大一次会议收到的议案中，建议制定“检察公益诉讼法”的有17件，占全部议案的6.3%；699名代表参与提出议案，占全体代表的23.5%。制定检察公益诉讼法已纳入全国人大常委会立法计划。目前，全国人大监察司法委启动了法律草案研究起草工作。

5 上级检察院统一调用辖区检察人员办案制度

人民检察院组织法第二十四条规定，上级检察院“可以统一调用辖区的检察人员办理案件”。2023年9月，经全国人大常委会法工委同意，最高人民检察院印发规范性文件，明确调用方式包括：调用本院检察人员到辖区的下级检察院办理案件；调用辖区的下级检察院检察人员到本院办理案件；调用辖区的下级检察院检察人员到辖区的其他下级检察院办理案件。被调用检察人员以检察官身份代表办理案件的检察院履行出庭支持公诉等职责的，该院按照法定程序提请本级人大常委会任命为本院的检察员，任命前可以以检察官助理身份协助办理案件。

6 法治督察

系各级党委法治建设决策议事协调机构的一项基本职责，主要目的是督促落实党中央关于全面依法治国的决策部署。中央层面法治督察工作，由中央全面依法治国委员会办公室（设在司法部）在中央全面依法治国委员会领导下开展。2023 年 12 月，最高人民检察院与司法部举行工作会商，明确共同探索建立法律监督与法治督察衔接配合机制：对法治督察中发现的需检察机关开展法律监督的问题线索，及时移送检察机关依法处理；对法律监督中发现的法治建设问题，可作为线索纳入法治督察工作安排。

Work Report of the Supreme People's Procuratorate

Delivered at the Second Session of the 14th National People's Congress of the People's Republic of China on March 8, 2024

Ying Yong

Attorney-General of the Supreme People's Procuratorate

Fellow Deputies,

On behalf of the Supreme People's Procuratorate (SPP), I will now present a report on its work for your deliberation and also for the opinions of the members of the National Committee of the Chinese People's Political Consultative Conference (CPPCC).

2023 Work Review

In 2023, under the strong leadership of the Party Central Committee with Comrade Xi Jinping at the core, and under the strong supervision of the National People's Congress (NPC) and its Standing Committee, the SPP adhered to the guidance of Xi Jinping Thought on Socialism with Chinese Characteristics for a New Era. We fully implemented the spirit of the 20th National Congress and the Second Plenary Session of the 20th Central Committee of the Communist Party of China (CPC), and earnestly implemented the resolutions of the First Session of the 14th NPC. We deeply comprehended the decisive significance of the Two Establishments, strengthened our commitment to the Four Consciousnesses, the Four-Sphere Confidence and the Two Upholds. We have actively integrated and served the Chinese path to modernization, faithfully performed the legal supervision duties entrusted by the Constitution and laws by handling every case with high quality and efficiency, consciously serving the overall situation, delivering justice for the people, and upholding for rule of law as well as firmly advancing the procuratorial practice of

Xi Jinping thought on the Rule of Law, achieving new progress in all aspects of procuratorial work. Procuratorial organs nationalwide handled a total of 4.253 million cases, up 28.9% year on year .

I. Serving the overall situation and fully performing the procuratorial functions to maintain stability and promote development

Closely aligning with the central tasks of the Party and the state in the New Era and on the new journey, the nation's procuratorial organs implemented the holistic view of national security, respected and protected human rights, and effectively performed legal supervision duties, to better serve both high-quality development and a high-level of security.

Resolutely safeguarding national security and social stability. Punishing crimes in accordance with law is a basic duty of the procuratorial organs in maintaining social stability. Over the past year, arrests were approved for 726 000 suspects and 1 688 000 people were prosecuted, up 47.1% and 17.3% year on year respectively. "Strict" deterrence was maintained against serious crimes. The procuratorial organs nationalwide strictly cracked down on activities of infiltration, destruction, subversion and separatism by hostile forces in accordance with the law. We promoted long-term stability and peace in regions such as Xinjiang by integrating the fight against terrorism and separatism with promoting the legalization and normalization of efforts to maintain stability. We thoroughly advanced the normalization of the action against gang crimes and organized crimes, prosecuting 15 000 people. We strictly punished serious violent crimes such as intentional homicide, robbery and kidnapping in accordance with the law, prosecuting 61 000 people. We focused on punishing crimes on which the public has given strong feedback, such as theft, fraud and drug crimes, prosecuting 350 000 people. Cooperating with the public security organs to tackle a backlog of homicide cases, the SPP lawfully approved the pursuit of 137 homicide cases that happened more than 20 years ago, including the case of Jiang Sixing and Xue Sanyuan's killing of crew members, ensuring that justice will be achieved regardless of time and distance.

Combining leniency and severity to promote crime governance. The procuratorial organs nationalwide comprehensively and accurately implemented the criminal policy of combining leniency and severity, being strict or lenient as called for, so that the punishments suit the crimes. Decisions to not arrest were made for 266 000 people suspected of committing crimes where arrest was not necessary; and decisions to not prosecute were made for 498 000 people where the circumstances of the crimes were slight and criminal punishment was unnecessary or could be waived in accordance with the law; up 22.5% and 12.6% year on year respectively. We worked with the Ministry of Public Security to formulate regulations on reviewing the necessity of detention, and changed the compulsory measures for 29 000 suspects where it was not necessary to continue detention in accordance with the law. The lenient system of taking pleas was applied in accordance with the law, with over 90% of suspects taking pleas in the procuratorial stage, and the rate of parties' acceptance of first instance trial verdicts was 96.8%, 36% higher than in cases in which the system had not been applied. In collabration with the Supreme People's Court (SPC), the Ministry of Public Security and the Ministry of Justice, special opinions were formulated to unify national law enforcement and judicial standards for drunk driving so as to form a governance system for drunk driving that bridges administrative penalties and criminal prosecution.

Fully performing procuratorial duties to fight against corruption. The procuratorial organs nationalwide accepted the transfer of 20 000 people involved in duty crimes from the supervision commissions at all levels, up 9.3% year on year; 18 000 people have been prosecuted, including 25 former provincial and ministerial level cadres. Strengthening cooperation and constraint, early involvement work was jointly regulated with the National Supervisory Commission, and cases with early procuratorate involvement accounted for 61.1% of all cases accepted; with supplementary investigation being carried out by the procuratorate itself in 3 020 cases and 808 cases being returned for supplementary investigation. Actively participating in the governance of industry-centered and systemic corruption, we prosecuted 348 and 580 people for duty crimes in the financial and medical fields respectively, and guided the Hubei procuratorial organs in handling a series of corruption cases in the football sector, indicting Chen Xuyuan, former chairman of Chinese Football Association, and 14 others. By jointly investigating the taking and offering of bribes, we prosecuted 2 593 people for bribery crimes, up 18.9% year on year. Cooperating in tracking fugitives and stolen assets, we applied to the court to confiscate the unlawful gains of 14 embezzlement and bribery suspects who had absconded or died. Xu Guojun, former director of Kaiping Branch of Bank of China, who embezzled and misappropriated huge amounts of public funds before fleeing abroad for 20 years, was forcibly repatriated after continuous pursuit, and sentenced to life imprisonment after being prosecuted by the Guangdong procuratorial organs in accordance with the law, a demonstration of our firm determination to pursue all fugitives.

Striving to create a business environment under the rule of law. The rule of law is the best environment for business. Focusing on using rule of law methods to stabilize social expectations and bolster market confidence, 121 000 people were prosecuted for crimes that disrupt the order of the market economy, up 20.4% year on year. 9 428 people were prosecuted for crimes that endanger tax collection and administration, such as falsely issuing special invoices for value-added tax and fraudulently obtaining export tax refunds, up 10.9% year on year. All types of business entities were shown equal treatment and protection in accordance with the law. In order to promote optimization of the environment to develop the private economy, we formulated procuratorial opinions to promote the development and growth of the private economy by strictly distinguishing economic disputes from economic crimes, administrative violations from criminal offenses, and crimes by units from crimes by individuals; continuing to clean up "pinned cases" involving enterprises, resolutely correcting the use of criminal means to intervene in civil and economic disputes, and resolutely correcting the sealing, seizure, and freezing of property exceeding the scope and time limit. In response to the infringement of enterprises' interests by key persons in private enterprises, such as by embezzlement, misappropriation of funds and the acceptance of bribes, 12 procuratorial measures have been introduced to promote the improvement of internal anti-corruption mechanisms in private enterprises and to lawfully protect enterprises' property rights and entrepreneurs' rights and interests.

Ensuring innovation and driving development. 45 measures were introduced on the procuratorial organs handling intellectual property cases, strengthening comprehensive protection. 18 000 people were prosecuted for crimes such as trademark, patent, copyright and trade secrets infringement, up 40.8% year on year. Protections for trade secrets in the litigation process were strengthened to prevent “secondary leakage”. 2 508 cases supervising civil and administrative intellectual property litigation were handled, which was 2.7 times higher than that in 2022. The procuratorial organs nationalwide handled 873 cases of public interest litigation in the field of intellectual property. A special supervision program was carried out on malicious litigation involving intellectual property. For example, a certain cultural media company posed as the copyright owner of music and television works and filed more than 5 800 malicious suits; and the SPP listed it as under supervision, guided the procuratorial organs of nine provinces and cities, including Guangdong and Shandong, to simultaneously supervise retrials in the courts in accordance with the law, and approved the arrest of five suspects, which promoted the creation of a good innovation ecology.

Resolutely maintaining financial security. We formulated 23 procuratorial opinions to ensure the high-quality development of finance, strictly combating financial crimes, and preventing and mitigating financial risks. The procuratorial organs nationalwide prosecuted 27 000 people for financial fraud and crimes that disrupted financial management order, including 18 000 people for fundraising fraud and illegal absorption of public savings, maintained a state of high pressure for punishing financial crimes related to the public, and made every effort to recover losses. Coordinating to improve the law enforcement and judicial standards for securities crimes, the SPP listed major cases for supervision and prosecuted 346 people for securities crimes such as fraudulent issuance of securities, insider trading, and market manipulation, with jointly preserving the security of capital market and the legitimate rights and interests of small and medium-sized investors. We collaborated with the State Administration of Foreign Exchange to publish typical cases and sternly crack down on illegal activities related to foreign exchange. We strengthened cooperation with the supervision commissions and public security organs at all levels on anti-money laundering, prosecuting 2 971 people for money laundering crimes, up 14.9% year on year. For example, Xiang helped others conceal or hide criminal proceeds by purchasing "virtual currency" at a high price and selling it cheaply to overseas traders, illegally remitting more than 1.8 billion yuan abroad, and the Shanghai procuratorial organs initiated a public prosecution against them in accordance with the law, demonstrating that we will never allow "black money" to be laundered into "white".

Promoting the governance of cyberspace in accordance with the law. The SPP formulated 21 guidelines for the procuratorial organs on governing cyberspace in accordance with the law, and the procuratorial organs nationalwide prosecuted 323 000 people for committing crimes by using the internet, up 36.2% year on year. In order to resolutely punish online violence that "cuts with a keystroke", we collaborated with the SPC and the Ministry of Public Security to formulate guiding opinions, and lawfully prosecuted and pursued the criminal liability of those suspected of crimes such as recklessly spreading rumors, online defamation, abuse and insult, and "Doxxing", to preserve citizen's personality rights and interests, and online order. We purified the online public opinion environment by strictly cracking down on violations and crimes such as "online trolls" spreading rumors and manipulating traffic or extortion through public opinion. We punished telecommunication fraud and online gambling in accordance with the law, actively participating in the special action to combat telecommunications network fraud related to northern Myanmar by unearthing and cracking down on organizers, leaders, and "financiers" behind the scenes, prosecuting 51 000 people for telecommunication network fraud crimes, 147 000 people for assisting information network crimes, and 19 000 people for online gambling crimes, up 66.9%, 13%, and 5.3% year on year respectively. Targeting disorder in the internet field such as the infringement of personal information, false promotion, and consumer fraud, the procuratorial organs nationalwide handled 6 766 public interest litigation cases to spur the implementation of regulatory and platform responsibility by using the force of rule of law to maintain a clean and orderly internet environment.

Promoting social governance. We carried forward the core socialist values and promoted the building of a society governed by rule of law in performing our duties and handling cases. We continued to guide the idea of justified defense, concluding through review that 261 people had engaged in justified defense and would not be arrested or prosecuted in accordance with the law, up 25.5% year on year. For example, where the owner of a fast food restaurant fought and killed the thug who broke into the restaurant with a knife demanding money, or the manager of a game room injured a drunken troublemaker with a knife while stopping him, the procuratorial organs determined that they did not constitute a crime, as "the legal cannot yield to the illegal". We persisted in having the punishment fits the crime, seeking the "greatest common denominator" of fairness and justice within the legal framework. Where the vice dean of a certain school sexually assaulted an underage girl, and the girl's enraged father beat him, causing a minor injury, and was suspected of a crime, the procuratorial organ, after comprehensive consideration, lawfully decided not to prosecute the attacker in light of his reason for the incident, the minor circumstance and his voluntary surrender; and also supervised the filing of a case to pursue the molester's criminal responsibility as he had only been given administrative detention, which thereby demonstrates the judicial force of uniting the law, reason and emotion. We persisted in treating both symptoms and root causes, issuing

39 000 procuratorial suggestions in combination with performing duties and handling cases. The SPP issued its 9th and 10th procuratorial suggestions to the National Food and Strategic Reserves Administration and China Grain Reserves Group Ltd. Cowpany respectively so as to prevent and controll duty-related crimes and jointly safeguard food security. In response to the problem of violating the personal rights of the elderly in elderly care institutions, we issued the 11th procuratorial suggestion to the Ministry of Civil Affairs to promote enhanced supervision. The Beijing procuratorate discovered the issue of tens of thousands of fake certificates for special operations while digging into and handling cases, and promoted the investigation and handling of 126 people who had produced and sold fake certificates, urged the authorities to implement regulatory responsibility, and traced and rectified 226 websites counterfeiting official websites of the state organs.

Serving the rural areas with comprehensive revitalization. We deployed the special services for the "three rural concerns" of agriculture, rural areas and farmers. We strived to maintain social harmony and stability in rural areas, and 604 people were prosecuted for their clan or gang crime in rural areas.

We punished the crime of producing and selling counterfeit and shoddy agricultural materials in accordance with the law and prosecuted 820 people; we guided the procuratorial organs of Jilin, Heilongjiang, Henan, and other regions in carrying out public interest litigation in the agricultural machinery field to maintain the safety of agricultural production. We protected the red line of farmland in accordance with the law, protecting the high-standard farmland, and prosecuting 2 883 people for the crime of illegal occupation of agricultural land and handling 9 753 public interest litigation cases related to land protection. In response to the pollution caused by discarded agricultural film scattered in fields, we guided the procuratorial organs in Jiangxi, Guizhou, Qinghai, Xinjiang and other regions to carry out special supervision to promote cleaning and recycling to protect the soil ecology. A judicial relief fund of 110 million yuan was distributed to 13 000 rural victims who were in financial difficulties due to the cases.

Strengthening judicial protection of historical and cultural heritage. We coordinated to carry out efforts to combat and prevent crimes related to cultural relics, with 2 089 people prosecuted for crimes such as stealing from and excavating ancient tombs and reselling cultural relics, up 37.4% year on year. 2 734 cases of public interest litigation were handled in the field of protecting historical and cultural heritage. In collaboration with the National Cultural Heritage Administration, typical cases were published on public interest litigation for punishing cultural relics crimes and protecting the Great Wall. Cooperation was strengthened with the Ministry of Housing and Urban-Rural Development to promote the protection and inheritance of urban and rural historical and cultural heritage. The SPP guided the procuratorial organs in Liaoning, Jiangxi, Guangxi, Chongqing and other regions to strengthen the public interest protection of red resources, and guided the procuratorial organs in Shanxi, Fujian, Hainan, Xizang, Qinghai and other regions to strengthen the public interest protection of grotto temple relics, cultural relics related to Taiwan, South China Sea cultural relics, traditional villages, and intangible cultural heritage, protecting the heritage of Chinese culture through the rule of law.

Serving regional coordinated development. The SPP deepened regional procuratorial cooperation better serving western development, the comprehensive revitalization of the

Northeast, the accelerated rise of the central region, and faster modernization of the eastern region. The SPP guided the procuratorial organs in Beijing, Tianjin and Hebei to optimize coordination measures to jointly promote the establishment of a business environment under the rule of law and regional governance of the ecology and environment, and to serve the high-standard and high-quality construction of the Xiong'an New Area. In Shanghai, Jiangsu, Zhejiang, and Anhui, we guided the procuratorial organs to improve the mechanisms for integrated performance of duties across regions. In Guangdong, we supported the procuratorial organs in providing services to ensure the construction of the Guangdong-Hong Kong-Macao Greater Bay Area. In Hainan, we guided the procuratorial organs to provide service supporting the establishment of the free trade port. Special opinions were drafted to serve and guarantee the establishment of the Chengdu-Chongqing twin city economic ring, and the construction of magnificent Guangxi in the New Era.

Serving high-level opening to the outside world. The nation's procuratorial organs handled 4 243 criminal cases involving foreign interests, and 220 criminal judicial assistance cases, in accordance with the law, equally protecting the legitimate rights and interests of Chinese and foreign parties and promoting the joint high-quality construction of the "Belt and Road" deeply and firmly. The SPP launched its official English website, held the Prosecutors General Conference of the Shanghai Cooperation Organization (SCO) Member States in Shaanxi, consolidated and deepened multilateral judicial cooperation mechanisms such as the China-ASEAN Prosecutors-General Conference, the BRICS Attorneys-General Meeting and the International Prosecutor's Association, and played a role as a training base for exchanges between prosecutors from China and ASEAN member states with telling the story of China's rule of law in the New Era well to support major-country diplomacy.

II. Safeguarding and improving the people's livelihood in the performance of procuratorial duties, to deliver justice for the people

We closely focused on implementing the people-centered philosophy of development, firmly established the ideas of thinking "acting as if I were the one filing a lawsuit" and "sitting firmly on the side of the people", and ensuring that the procuratorial power was exercised for the people and to the people's satisfaction.

Guarding the safety of the people. We actively participated in a special correction of production safety risks, listed major production safety accident cases for supervision, prosecuted 4 750 people for major at-fault accidents, dangerous operations, or other crimes, and handled 17 000 cases of public interest litigation in this field. Heilongjiang procuratorial organs carried out a special supervision action of public interest litigation for campus venue safety and urged the rectification of more than 5 500 latent dangers. The extent of combating the crimes of manufacturing and selling toxic and harmful foods and counterfeit or shoddy drugs was severely increased, resolutely giving heavy penalties in accordance with the law, and prosecuting 13 000 people, up 31.5% year on year. 24 000 public interest litigation cases were handled in the food and drug safety field, up 16.8% year on year. We cooperated to carry out a special rectification of road traffic safety, issuing 7 442 procuratorial suggestions to promote the correction of loopholes in driving qualification supervision and violations of height and speed limits. The continuous promotion of safe delivery with the State Post Bureau and other departments achieved results, with 3 139 people being prosecuted for crimes of shipping drugs, guns, ammunition, and explosives, down 36.3% year on year. We collaborated with the State Administration for Market Regulation and others on a special initiative to address issues in the medical and cosmetics industries such as the illegal practice of medicine, the manufacture and sale of counterfeit goods, and false promotions. The crime of intentionally injuring and harassing medical doctors was punished in accordance with the law, with 226 people being prosecuted, down 51.6% year on year. We cooperated in the rectification of fraud in the medical insurance field, protecting the people's "life-saving money" in accordance with the law.

Strengthening judicial protection of the ecology and environment. Collaborative efforts were made to rectify hazardous waste pollution and fraud by third-party environmental protection service institutions, with 3 831 people being prosecuted for the crime of environmental pollution, down 11.3% year on year. We intensified the punishment for crimes undermining the protection of resources, prosecuting 35 000 people, up 6.4% year on year. 84 000 public interest litigation cases were handled in the field of environmental resources. To implement the Yangtze River Protection Law, the SPP directly filed public interest litigation cases regarding ship pollution in the Yangtze River and its tributaries, and the procuratorial organs along the Yangtze River handled 575 related cases at the same time, promoting a fully closed cycle of ship pollutant receipt and disposal. We also implemented the Yellow River Protection Law, holding the first National Procuratorial Strategic Forum for Serving and Safeguarding the Yellow River, and carried out a special action for the protection of Yellow River basin water resources in collaboration with the Ministry of Water Resources. We cooperated with the National Forestry and Grassland Administration to effectively protect and govern forests, grasslands, wetlands and deserts. We cooperated with the China Coast Guard on a special rectification of illegal sea sand mining. We guided the procuratorial organs of Hebei, Inner Mongolia, Heilongjiang, Jilin and other areas in special supervision items on the control of alien species, the prevention and control of desertification and the protection of black land. We submitted a special report on procuratorial work related to the environment and resources to the Standing Committee of the NPC, receiving robust oversight and strong support.

Lawfully resolving conflicts and disputes involving law and litigation. Upholding and developing the "Fengqiao Experiences" in the New Era, we solidly promoted the legalization of procuratorial xinfang work. We deployed a three-year campaign to tackle the root causes of xinfang disputes. Leading cadres of procuratorates at all levels handled 46 000 cases of xinfang. 1 062 cases of repeated xinfang were investigated and handed over and 1 024 have already been resolved. In collaboration with the judicial administrative organs, the SPP and the procuratorial organs of seven provinces, autonomous regions and municipalities, including Shandong and Ningxia, carried out pilot projects in which the first time applicants for review criminal case outcomes who request state compensation are to be represented by the public interest lawyers free of charge. We have responded to the public's xinfang in each case and received 886 000 cases of xinfang from the public, 99.8% were procedurally responded to within 7 days and 97.3% were given a processing or outcome response within 3 months.

Protecting the healthy growth of minors. There was "zero tolerance" for crimes against minors such as sexual assault, injury, and abuse, prosecuting 67 000 people, up 14.9% year on year. The policy of education, persuasion, and rescue for minors involved in crimes was adhered to, with 31 000 people given conditional non-prosecution for minor crimes and prosecuting 39 000 people for serious crimes in accordance with the law. We strengthened the prevention of juvenile delinquency, promoted graded interventions for delinquent minors, coordinated and promoted the construction of specialized schools in Hebei, Guangdong, Guangxi, Guizhou and Yunnan, to educate and correct minors with serious misconduct in accordance with the law. In collaboration with the All-China Women's Federation and others, typical cases on family education guidance and 57 000 guardianship exhortation orders were issued. In joint action with the administrative departments of education, 2 120 Practice Bases for Youth Legal Education were jointly established, and a cooperative mechanism was established to ensure that minors involved in cases remain in school and continue their studies. We promoted the implementation of the system for requesting information on people taking positions in units that have close contact with minors and the mandatory reporting system for violations against minors. We issued guiding cases on the protection of minors online, severely punished crimes such as "remote indecency" and violations that start online and move offline, and coordinated the prevention of Internet addiction and guided the safe use of the Internet. We promoted the resolution of challenges in the protection of minors in new forms of business, encouraging the regulatory departments to improve regulatory systems for e-sports hotels, the mystery box market, mystery role-playing, and escape room games. We optimized the overall performance of procuratorial duties, joining hands with all parties to provide a rule of law environment for the healthy growth of the children.

Safeguarding the lawful rights and interests of women in accordance with the law. We made allocations to comprehensively strengthen judicial protections for women's rights and interests. Crimes of infringing upon women's lives, health, and personal dignity were severely punished in accordance with the law, with 46 000 people being prosecuted, up 10.7% year on year. A criminal suspect who posted a secretly filmed video of a woman online was prosecuted for criminal insult by the Jiangsu procuratorial organs. 563 people were prosecuted for domestic violence. A special project was carried out with the All-China Women's Federation to provide judicial relief to 23 000 women who had suffered from criminal or civil infringement and were unable to obtain effective compensation through litigation and faced urgent difficulties in their lives. We deepened public interest litigation to protect women's rights and interests, focusing on supervising illegal acts such as employment discrimination and demeaning women's character in handling 1 490 related public interest litigation cases. We issued typical cases on protecting rural women's legitimate rights and interests related to land in accordance with the law. In collaboration with the Ministry of Human Resources and Social Security, the National Health Commission, the All-China Federation of Trade Unions and others, we issued norms and guidelines to promote the improvement of systems for special labor protections for female workers and the elimination of workplace sexual harassment. Dedicated reception windows were opened in the four levels of procuratorate to establish "green channels" for the special protection of women's and children's rights and interests.

Protecting the legitimate rights and interests of specified groups in accordance with the law. In collaboration with the Ministry of Civil Affairs, the Ministry of Housing, Urban-Rural Development and the China Disabled Persons' Federation, we issued two sets of typical cases on protecting disabled persons' rights and interests, such as for employment, education and rehabilitation, in accordance with the law. 1 983 cases of public interest litigation were handled in the field of barrier-free environment construction so that there are no "barriers" to love, and everyone can share in a better life. Regarding the impact on medicine safety from medicines' instructions with "print as small as ants", we guided the procuratorial organs in Jiangsu, Shanghai and other regions to use public interest litigation to promote reforms for the elderly such as large-print or simplified editions; the Tianjin procuratorial organs promoted the addition of voice station announcement functions in public transportation software; Hubei procuratorial organs promoted the addition of text alert functions in emergency calls to ensure the convenient integration of elderly and disabled persons into public life. We actively participated in the management of arrears of wages, issued typical cases of punishing malicious arrears of wages, prosecuted 1 082 people and recovered 380 million yuan from arrears of wages. To ensure that the citizens enjoy and effectively exercise their litigation rights in accordance with the law, we supported 77 000 civil lawsuits by migrant workers, disabled persons, and elderly people whose rights and interests were infringed, but who were unable to sue due to economic difficulties or lack of legal knowledge, up 16.8% year on year.

Resolutely guarding "Military Green" (representing national defense) and "Martyr Red" (symbolizing heroes and martyrs). We punished the crimes of endangering national defense interests and infringing upon the legitimate rights and interests of servicemen, military families, heroes and martyrs in accordance with the law, prosecuting 364 people, up 7. 1% year on year. We handled 1 202 cases of public interest litigation in the fields of national defense, military affairs and the protection of servicemen's rights and interests. We continued to promote the special supervision project on military airfield clearance and the protection of military ports and ship navigation channels. We collaboratively strengthened the prevention and control of security risks at military training grounds to prevent the illegal excavation, collection, and sale of unexploded ordnance from interfering with combat readiness training and endangering public safety. We coordinated and carried out the special action of "Guarding Military Uniforms", punishing the crime of illegal production or sale of military uniforms in accordance with the law. We assisted 1 331 servicemen, military families, and veterans who suffered from illegal infringement. 875 public interest litigation cases were handled in the field of protecting the rights and interests of heroes and martyrs. In regards to the problem of inadequate management and protection of some remote tombs of martyrs, Shandong procuratorial organs joined hands with veterans' affairs departments to carry out special activities for three consecutive years, urging the centralized relocation or local protection of 5 326 sites. In response to three online bloggers maliciously producing and disseminating false videos, defaming a founding major general as a traitor, the local and military procuratorates in Zhejiang cooperated to file civil public interest litigation in accordance with the law, and ordered them to publicly apologize and bear liability for compensating the harm to the public interest because the honor of heroes cannot be desecrated.

Effectively safeguarding the legitimate rights and interests of compatriots from Hong Kong, Macao and Taiwan, overseas Chinese, returned overseas Chinese and their family members. Cases involving Hong Kong, Macao, Taiwan and overseas Chinese were handled in accordance with the law. High-level exchanges and practical cooperation were deepened with the judicial organs of Hong Kong and Macao and the ICAC, and training courses were made available to judicial and legal professionals in Hong Kong and Macao. We joined with the Federation of Overseas Chinese to guide cooperation between overseas Chinese and provincial level procuratorates, and escorted the development of overseas Chinese enterprises and safeguarded the rights and interests of overseas Chinese. We guided Fujian's procuratorial organs to formulate opinions serving the construction of integrated cross-straits development demonstration zones so as to provide high-quality legal services to Taiwan compatriots and enterprises.

III. Stepping forward for the rule of law and promoting social fairness and justice through procuratorial supervision

We closely focused on the goal of "striving to make the people feel fairness and justice in every judicial case" and making the "high-quality and efficient handling of every case" become the basic values and aspiration in performing procuratorial duties in the New Era and new journey, ensuring that fairness and justice were realized in substance, making fairness and justice better and more quickly manifest in procedure, so that the people may feel, can feel, and do feel fairness and justice in the effects.

Deepening supervision of the filing, investigation and adjudication of criminal cases. We improved mechanisms for investigation supervision and coordinated cooperation with the Ministry of Public Security, the Ministry of State Security, the General Administration of Customs and China Coast Guard. We supervised case filing and the withdrawal of 139 000 cases where the investigative organs should have filed cases but did not, or filed cases that should not have been filed, up 68.2% year on year. Where a crime was not constituted or the evidence was insufficient, decisions were made not to approve the arrest of 210 000 people and not to prosecute 54 000 people in accordance with the law, up 51.1% and 10.4% year on year respectively; an additional 19 000 people were arrested and another 99 000 people were prosecuted where there should have been arrested or prosecuted but arrest was not requested or the case was not transferred for prosecution, up 12.8% and 66% year on year respectively. There were 7 876 procuratorial appeals submitted against criminal judgments that were found to be truly in error, of which the courts have concluded 6 114 cases, including 4 885 cases of revised judgments or remands for retrial, with a change rate of 79.9%. For example, Chen Cang killed persons to silence them after he was discovered burglarizing a building with others, and was caught 17 years after the crime was committed. Because he recanted his confession, the original court found that there was a conflict in the evidence and acquitted him, but after examination, the SPP found that the existing evidence already formed a complete chain sufficient to eliminate reasonable doubt, and raised a procuratorial appeal in accordance with the law, and the judgment was changed to a suspended death sentence.

When examining the case of "a rape and homicide committed by Mr. Mao", the Sichuan procuratorial organs found that the objective evidence could not confirm that he did the crime and that the real offender was someone else, so it urged the public security organs to release him in accordance with the law and continued to follow up and oversee the case, capturing the real offender 14 years later. Let the guilty be punished and the innocent be cleared so as to demonstrate the rule of law and justice.

Strengthening supervision of criminal enforcement. The SPP has organized the drafting of a three-year plan for inspection circuits, directly conducted inspection circuits of four prisons and four detention centers, and piloted inspection circuits on community corrections in nine provinces, autonomous regions and cities, including Fujian, Henan, Chongqing and Gansu. In collaboration with the SPC, Ministry of Justice and others, we formulated the guiding opinions on promoting the application of parole in accordance with the law and on regulating the enforcement of temporary service of sentences outside prison, by which we not only supervised and corrected "the service of sentences on paper only" and "buying one's way out prison", but also prevented failures to reduce sentences where they should be reduced, and failures to release those who should be released. The acceptance of supervision cases of commutation, parole and temporary service of sentences outside prison rose by 25.2% year on year; and 26 000 procuratorial opinions were submitted regarding improper requests, decisions or rulings. We urged 3 652 people to return to prison for enforcement where the conditions for outside enforcement no longer existed. We also strengthened the supervision of the enforcement of property penalties, submitting 95 000 corrective opinions and promoting the enforcement against 670 million yuan.

Improving the supervision of civil proceedings. 14 000 procuratorial suggestions for appeal or retrial were submitted regarding civil judgments found to be truly in error, and the trial of 8 537 cases has already concluded in the courts, including 7 549 cases where the judgment was changed, remanded for retrial, or withdrawn after mediation and reconciliation, with a change rate of 88.4%. The SPP submitted appeals against 41 typical cases. In collaboration with the SPC, we standardized the handling of cases suggested by the procurators for civil retrial and strengthened supervision by the same level. 130 000 procuratorial suggestions were made on illegal situations in civil trial and enforcement activities. We strengthened legal interpretation and reasoning in 55 000 cases where applications for supervision were not supported to ensure judicial authoritativeness. We carried out supervision of fraudulent litigation, correcting 9 359 cases in accordance with the law, and prosecuting 925 people for fraudulent litigation crimes. Where a criminal organization had judicial staff "in their pocket" and used fake lawsuits to evade debts, Liaoning procuratorial organs urged the correction of 184 related cases while concurrently punishing crimes involving criminal gangs and their "protective umbrella" in accordance with the law.

Strengthening supervision of administrative litigation. 624 procuratorial appeals or suggestions for retrial of administrative judgments found to be in error were submitted, with 305 having concluded trial in the courts, of which 231 cases had judgments changed, were remand for retrial, or were withdrawn after mediation and settlement, with a change rate of 75.7%. 45 000 procuratorial suggestions were made on illegal situations in administrative trial and enforcement activities. In collaboration with relevant departments, 22 000 cases of administrative disputes were substantively resolved, among them, 780 cases have been disputed for more than ten years. For example, two groups of villagers in a certain county in Hunan had disputes over the ownership of mountains, forests, farmland and land, but would not accept administrative decisions and would not carry out administrative judgments, leading to criminal sentencing of 18 people following four armed fights. After accepting the application for supervision, the procuratorates at the municipal and county levels, together with the local government, guided the villagers from confrontation to dialogue, and the disputes that had lasted for more than 20 years were eventually resolved.

Promoting the organic connection between procuratorial supervision and administrative enforcement of law. We explored the supervision of illegal administrative acts and put forward 32 000 procuratorial suggestions on the administrative organs' illegal exercise of authority, or failure to exercise authority, which were found in the performance of legal supervision duties, up 50.2% year on year. The pilot program of procuratorial supervision over compulsory isolated drug rehabilitation was deepened, putting forward 2 036 procuratorial suggestions. We promoted the two-way connection between administrative enforcement of law and criminal justice, urged the organs of administrative enforcement of law to transfer 5 869 suspected criminal cases, and prevented administrative penalties from being used in place of criminal penalties. We put forward prosecution opinions on non-prosecuted person who should be subject to administrative penalties, and transferred to the competent authority for handling 113 000 people to prevent them from no punishment.

Deepening procuratorial public interest litigation. The system of procuratorial public interest litigation is an original achievement of Xi Jinping Thought on the Rule of Law in the field of public interest protection. Keeping in mind the sacred duty of being "representatives of the public interest", we filed and handled 190 000 cases of public interest litigation, including 168 000 cases of administrative public interest litigation. We issued 116 000 pre-litigation procuratorial suggestions to the administrative organs with a reply and rectification rate of 99.1%, and the vast majority of issues with public interest harms were resolved before litigation. For those that were still not resolved after an announcement or procuratorial suggestion was issued, 13 000 lawsuits were filed in accordance with the law, and 99.96% were supported by the judgment. We improved the mechanism for the connection and transfer between the people's congress deputies' suggestions, CPPCC proposals, and procuratorial public interest litigation, and worked with the United Front Work Department of the Central Committee and each democratic party's center to jointly build the "Yixin Weigong" procuratorate public interest volunteer cloud platform. In one case, some volunteers reported that the fire extinguishers purchased online weren't able to put out fires, and the procuratorial organs of Anhui found that such extinguishers did have major potential safety hazards, and so they made the procuratorial suggestions to urge the competent authorities to make special rectification and strengthen supervision, seized millions of fake and inferior extinguishers and arrested 22 people involved. The Standing Committee of the NPC has included the formulation of the Procuratorial Public Interest Litigation Law in its legislative plan, and the SPP is actively cooperating to bring the "China Plan" for judicial protection of the public interest into the law.

Increasing the force of procuratorial investigation work. The procuratorial investigation is an important function entrusted to the procuratorial organs by law. Investigations were initiated in accordance with the law for 1 976 people relating to crimes committed by judicial staff members exploiting their authority, which were discovered during litigation supervision, such as bending the law for personal gain, abusing power, and extorting confessions by torture, up 36.5% year on year. Ten years ago, four prison police beat a prisoner to death and lied that he had died of illness, and his family members made accusations for many years with no effect. The SPP discovered and transferred leads during its circuit inspections, and the Gansu procuratorial organs filed a case for investigation, with all four people being sentenced to fixed-term imprisonment. Investigations were initiated in accordance with the law for 176 people relating to major crimes committed by state organ staff members exploiting their authority, that were under the jurisdiction of public security organs but needed to be directly accepted by the procuratorate. A deputy director of a certain police station collaborated with others to organize blackmail, and the Hunan procuratorial organs initiated an investigation and prosecuted 8 people who were pursued for criminal responsibility in accordance with the law. Judicial corruption seriously damages judicial justice and impacts judicial credibility, and must be severely punished in accordance with the law.

Digital procuracy enabling legal supervision. We formulated a digital procuracy plan and built a working mechanism for "business leadership, data integration, technical support and emphasizing application". Tianjin procuratorial organs developed supervision models for tax fraud cases, screening more than 10 000 items of abnormal data such as false declaration of goods' names, false increases of product quantities, and false collections and settlement of foreign exchanges, then transferred these to relevant departments for investigation and punishment and used procuratorial suggestions to urge the administrative organs to plug loopholes, strengthen oversight and recover losses. The procuratorial organs in areas such as Beijing, Shanxi, Zhejiang and Sichuan have developed big data application models for legal supervision such as the illegal use of public rental housing, failures to reclaim land when temporary-uses expired, false detection reports issued by intermediary institutions and illegal extraction of urban groundwater, so as to promote systemic governance and safeguard the public interest.

IV. Accepting the people's oversight, ensuring the correct exercise of procuratorial power in accordance with the law

The supervisors should be more receptive to supervision, who should perform their duties under the supervision of the people in accordance with the law.

Consciously accepting the oversight of the NPC. We deeply studied and implemented the spirit of the first session of the 14th NPC and organized the four levels of procuratorates to uniformly implement it. 95 NPC deputies were invited to serve as the new special supervisors. We invited 1715 participant attendances by NPC deputies in procuratorial work inspections and activity engagements; We visited 2 239 NPC deputies to hear their opinions in person. We carefully studied the 3 016 opinions and suggestions put forward by the NPC deputies in their deliberation reports and research discussions, implementing them one by one and responding to them individually. We earnestly addressed the

230 written suggestions put forward by NPC deputies and turned them into practical measures for improving work. The standing committees of provincial people's congresses in Inner Mongolia, Jiangsu, Anhui, Guizhou, Shaanxi and other provinces made decisions specifically to strengthen legal supervision and procuratorial suggestions, effectively ensuring that the procuratorial organs perform their duties in accordance with the law.

Consciously accepting the democratic oversight. 296 participant attendances by members of the CPPCC were invited to engaged in special research, public hearings, and other activities. The SPP earnestly handled 72 proposals put forward by members of the CPPCC, and organized special procurators to conduct special research on the procuratorial work of public interest litigation. We strengthened regular contact with democratic parties, federations of industry and commerce, and persons without party affiliations, to report on work and hear their opinions and suggestions. We deepened cooperation with the All-China Federation of Industry and Commerce, jointly holding a summit on the construction of rule of law in the private economy and a special open day activity for private entrepreneurs, to jointly promote the healthy development of private economy.

Consciously accepting restraints on the performance of duties. We comprehensively reviewed cases where public security organs requested reconsideration or reexamination of decisions not to approve arrest or prosecute. We reviewed each case of public prosecution where the courts pronounced not guilty and implemented accountability. Annual exchange and consultation mechanisms were separately established with both the SPC and the Ministry of Justice. An annual four-party consultation mechanism with the SPC, Ministry of Justice, and All China Lawyers Association was also established. In collaboration with the Ministry of Justice and the National Lawyers Association, we formulated ten opinions on safeguarding the practice rights of lawyers and jointly oversaw their implementation, correcting 2 355 cases where law enforcement and judicial personnel infringed on the lawyers' practice rights, up 32.3% year on year.

Consciously accepting social oversight. We fully disclosed the process and outcomes of handling cases to the parties involved, promptly disclosed the handling of important cases and procuratorial legal documents to the public, and released procuratorial case data and typical cases every quarter. We conducted open hearings on procuratorial work, and invited deputies of the NPC and local people's congress, members of the CPPCC, and experts and scholars to participate in the evaluation of controversial and influential cases such as reviews for arrest, proposed non-prosecutions, xinfang, and appeals, to help the parties resolve "legal issues" and "emotional entanglements". A total of 258 000 hearings were held, up 22.1% year on year, with a resolution rate of 78.6% for xinfang cases after a hearing. We normalized carrying out procuratorial open day activities. The people's supervisors supervised the procuratorates to handle 248 000 cases, up 96.1% year on year. We quickly verified and promptly responded to media reports involving the procuratorate, sincerely accepting their oversight. The procuratorial power has being operated in sunshine, promoting fairness and winning public trust through openness.

V. Strengthen our own establishment and forging an invincible procuratorial army for the New Era

We implemented the requirement of comprehensive and

strict governance of the Party, formulated and implemented opinions on the construction of the procuratorial team for the New Era, and forged a loyal, clean and responsible procuratorial team.

Deepening thematic education. We firmly grasped the overall requirements of "studying the thought, strengthening party spirit, emphasizing practice, and making new contributions", to thoroughly study, think, practice, and understand Xi Jinping Thought on Socialism with Chinese Characteristics for a New Era; firmly supporting the Two Establishments and firmly achieving the Two Upholds as the bright political background for the procuratorial organs on the new journey in the New Era. We continued to strengthen political construction, formulate methods for evaluating political caliber, and organize political rotation training, so as to continuously improve the political acumen, understanding and capacity to deliver. We strengthened the construction of procuratorial culture, and promoted the spirit of procuratorial models, commending 38 national model procuratorates and 59 national model procurators such as Ma Weiwei and Qu Xin, cultivating the procuratorial spirit in the New Era of "loyalty, serving the people, responsibility, justice and integrity", making seeking truth and being pragmatic with taking responsibility and working hard the distinctive characteristics of the procuratorial personnel in performing their duties.

Strengthening the construction of professional competence. We formulated a five-year plan for procuratorial education and training, and regularly conducted joint training for procurators, law enforcement, judicial personnel, and lawyers in the same classroom. We selected 49 national procuratorial experts and held competitions such as a national competition for the top ten procurators to cultivate leading talent in procuratorial operations. 28 judicial interpretations and documents of a similar nature were formulated, and 33 guiding cases were released. We deepened cooperation with schools, inviting 11 experts and scholars to take temporary posts in the SPP, organizing 106 procuratorial practice experts to go onto campuses, selecting 180 procuratorial practice courses for classrooms, and jointly building 38 procuratorial research bases, which has promoted the integration and mutual promotion of theoretical research and practical application of Xi Jinping Thought on the Rule of Law.

Strengthening the management of procuratorial business. We formulated the opinions on accelerating the modernization of the management of procuratorial business for the New Era, improving guidance systems, evaluation systems, and constraint and supervision systems for procuratorial business, following judicial logic, guiding the establishment of a correct view of political achievement, planning "quantity with quality" and "quality with quantity" with a greater emphasis on quality. The quality and efficiency of legal supervision work significantly improved: as compared with 2022, the average time of the review for prosecution in individual cases decreased by 4.8 days, and post-arrest acquittals and waivers of criminal punishment decreased by 24.8%, the number of criminal compensation cases accepted decreased by 30.5%, the percentage of procuratorial appeal cases resulting in a change increased by 6.3 points, and the number of xinfang over dissatisfaction with procuratorate's handling decisions decreased by 7.9%.

Deepening the comprehensive and coordinated reform of judicial system. We developed a five-year plan for procuratorial reform, clarifying 36 reform tasks. We improved the mechanism for integrated performance of duties with the support of the Legal Work Committee of the Standing Committee of the NPC, standardizing the system for higher-level procuratorates to uniformly mobilize the procuratorial personnel in their jurisdiction to handle cases. We deepened the differentiated management of procuratorial personnel, improving the system for selecting procurators and optimizing the training of procurator assistants. The chief procurators at the four levels of procuratorate regularly attended meetings of the trial committees of courts at the corresponding level. We promoted the establishment of linkage mechanisms between the law enforcement superversion of the Political and Legal Affairs Commissions of the Party Committees and the procuratorial organs' legal supervision in 15 provinces, regions and cities including Tianjin, Yunnan, Ningxia and Xinjiang.

Fully and accurately implementing the judicial responsibility system. We persisted in giving equal emphasis to decentralization and management and in combining case management with personnel management. We upheld the unity of highlighting the primary position of procurators in case handling and the leadership of the director in the procuratorate's work, and the director effectively took responsibility for "managing" the procurators to handle cases. We improved the system of punishment and protection of procurators' rights and interests. We focused on key stages, such as decisions not to approve arrest or prosecute in criminal cases, and appeals in civil cases, to further improve restraint and supervision mechanisms, both internally and externally, from top to bottom. We carried out special inspections on prominent issues in law enforcement and the judiciary, correcting problems in the performance of procuratorial duties, and promoting the fair, efficient, and clean operation of procuratorial authority in accordance with the law. We strengthened the supervision and management of cases handled by the SPP itself, and had a special action on cleaning up long-pending cases, with the superior procuratorates leading the subordinate ones in standardizing the performance of duties.

Deepening the comprehensive and strict management of the procuratorial team. Legal supervision organs should have courage and proclivity for supervision, and even more importantly, they should bravely supervise themselves. We persisted in keeping a stern tone with deepening the education and rectification of the cadre teams and resolutely preventing and controlling the “darkness under the lamp”. We shouldered the political responsibility of inspections within the system, with formulating a five-year plan and carrying out the first round of inspections of the leading Party members’ groups of provincial procuratorates. We analyzed and reported typical cases of procuratorial personnel’ violations of discipline and law so as to provide practical warnings and education based on the people and things around them. We continued to deepen the implementation of the “Three Provisions” on preventing interference in the judiciary, requiring that records must be made of every asking, that every case must be investigated, and that accountability must be pursued, and the procuratorial personnel recorded and reported 238 000 cases, up 40.8% year on year. We firmly supported the disciplinary inspection and supervision organs in enforcing discipline and accountability, and 3 persons from the SPP were investigated and punished for violating discipline and law; 413 persons from the local procuratorial organs were investigated and punished for using their procuratorial power to violate discipline and law, up 13.1% year on year, and of these, 78 persons were pursued for criminal liability, down 20.4% year on year.

Striving to consolidate the foundation of primary procuratorates. We firmly established a clear orientation for primary procuratorates, deepened the mechanism for leading cadres of higher procuratorates to contact primary procuratorates, and assisted local Party committees in coordinating and strengthening the leadership teams of primary procuratorates. The extent of training was increased, with the SPP directly training 21 000 procuratorial personnel from the primary procuratorates, including 685 directors of primary procuratorates. Together with the Ministry of Finance, standards were formulated for allocating equipment to primary procuratorates. We deepened assistance between procuratorial counterparts by organizing groups of lecturers to tour and teach in the western regions and sending 322 core operational personnel to Xizang, Xinjiang and Qinghai to support work there. Twenty chief procurators of primary procuratorates were selected to take temporary posts in the SPP, and 28 outstanding young cadres of the SPP were selected to "be cultivated" into talents in the primary procuratorates.

Fellow deputies, we have embarked on a new journey, while

the Party and state have had great achievements in their undertakings, the people's procuratorial career is steadily advancing. This is fundamentally due to the Comrade Xi Jinping's leadership and helmsmanship, and the scientific guidance of Xi Jinping Thought on Socialism with Chinese Characteristics for a New Era, and is also the result of strong oversight by the NPC and its Standing Committee, strong support from the State Council, democratic supervision from the CPPCC, the cooperation and restraint from the National Supervision Commission and the SPC, enthusiastic concern of all democratic parties, All-China Federation of Industry and Commerce, non-partisan individuals and people's organizations, and the support and assistance of the local Party and government organs at all levels, deputies, committee members and all sectors of society. On behalf of the SPP, I would like to express my sincere gratitude!

We are soberly aware that there are still many outstanding problems in the procuratorial work. Firstly, the use of Xi Jinping Thought on the Rule of Law to guide the performance of procuratorial duties still needs to be strengthened, the depth of integration into national governance and service towards high-quality development is insufficient, and we need to further strengthen procuratorial work that is for the people. Secondly, there are weak links in the fulfillment of legal supervision responsibilities, and the problems of insufficient supervision, ineffective supervision and inadequate supervision still exist. Administrative and civil procuratorial work are still weak with shortcomings. Thirdly, the idea and quality of supervision and handling of cases of the procuratorial personnel do not meet the people's higher requirements for fairness and justice, and the level of team specialization needs to be improved. Fourthly, some procuratorial policies and measures are not fully implemented at the primary procuratorates, whose primary work still needs to be strengthened. Fifthly, the comprehensive supporting reform of the judicial system still needs to be deepened, the mechanism for restricting and supervising the operation of procuratorial power still needs to be improved, and judicial injustice and judicial corruption still occur. We will take strong measures and strive to solve these problems.

2024 Work Plan

In 2024, the procuratorial organs nationalwide must adhere to the guidance of Xi Jinping Thought on Socialism with Chinese Characteristics for a New Era, and fully implement the spirit of the 20th National Congress of the CPC and the Second Plenary Session of the 20th CPC Central Committee. We must firmly support the Two Establishments and firmly achieve the Two Upholds as well as thoroughly implement *The Opinions of the CPC Central Committee on Strengthening the Legal Supervision by the Procuratorial Organs in the New Era.* Keeping a political perspective and focusing on the rule of law, we will handle every case with high quality and efficiency in order to ensure the unified and correct implementation of the nation's laws and continue to promote the procuratorial practice of Xi Jinping thought on the rule of law so as to support and serve the Chinese path to modernization through modernization of procuratorial work.

Firstly, we will always adhere to the Party's absolute leadership over procuratorial work. We will consciously integrate into the overall situation of the work of the Party and state, and ensure that procuratorial work will follow up wherever the Party's central work is promoted. We will strengthen the Party's political construction in the procuratorial organs, consolidate and expand on the achievements of thematic education, improve institutional mechanisms for the procuratorial organs to learn and implement the Party's innovative theory, and continue to promote the use of learning to shape the soul, enhance wisdow, correct the atmosphere and promote work. We will promote the deep integration of the Party's political construction and procuratorial operations, using Party construction to lead team development and promote the procuratorial business.

Secondly, we will resolutely safeguard national security, social stability and the people's tranquility. We will devote our full efforts to a higher level of Peaceful China Initiative, severely punish the crimes endangering national security, serious violent crimes, major drug crimes and serious economic crimes in accordance with the law so as to constantly enhance the people's sense of security. We will advance the normalization of the struggle to crackdown on gang-related crime in accordance with the law by striking early while crimes are small and striking accurately and firmly without lowering or increasing the standard. We will improve mechanisms for linking with supervision work to advance the fight against corruption. We will coordinate to carry out the "Clean Internet" campaign to crack down on online rumors, punish cybercrimes, and promote the administration and governance of the Internet in accordance with the law. We will thoroughly combat and rectify crimes of telecom and network fraud. We will give full play to the role of procuratorial suggestions in promoting the social governance. We will implement the responsibility system for popular legal education in which "all those who enforce the law, teach the law", combining case handling with strengthening legal publicity and education, and helping to accelerate the construction of a rule of law society. We will deepen cooperation between the military and civilian procuratorates, serve and promote the construction of strategic capacity in emerging fields in order to effectively safeguard national defense interests and the legitimate rights and interests of military personnel and their families, heroes and martyrs, civilian personnel in army and retired soldiers. We will strengthen foreign-related procuratorial work and deepen international procuratorial exchanges and cooperation so as to resolutely defending national sovereignty, security and development interests.

Thirdly, we will serve the absolute principle of high-quality development in this New Era in accordance with the law. We will completely and accurately implement the new concept of development, keeping in line with the orientation of macro policy, persisting in seeking progress while maintaining stability and promoting stability through progress, establishing the new before discarding the old, in order to provide the legal guarantees for China's economic recovery and long-term growth. We will carry out the special campaign of "procuratorates protecting enterprises", strengthening supervision of case-filing and investigation for enterprise-related economic crimes, strengthening the procuratorial supervision of enterprise-related civil and administrative cases, promoting the continuous optimization of the law-based business environment, and using the rule of law to enhance the confidence of enterprises in development. We will severely punish financial crimes to serve the high-quality financial development. We will enhance judicial implementation of the Anti-Monopoly Law and Anti-Unfair Competition Law to promote the building of a unified national market. We will strengthen judicial protection of intellectual property rights in key and core technologies and emerging industries, serving the development of the digital economy and accelerating the development of new-quality productive forces. We will strengthen procuratorial work on environment and resources to protect the blue skies, clear water and clean land. We will facilitate the prosperity and development of cultural affairs and industries to serve the construction of a strong cultural country. We will integrate into rural development with peace, rule of law and beauty, and serve the all-round revitalization of rural areas.

Fourthly, we will perform legal supervision duties with high quality and efficiency. We will adhere to the principle of performing our duties as a whole, comprehensively in accordance with the law, and promote the comprehensive, coordinated and full development of the four procuratorial functions in criminal, civil, administrative and public interest litigation. The procuratorial organs nationalwide will comprehensively strengthen legal supervision of litigation activities such as case filing, investigation, trial and enforcement with resolutely preventing and correcting wrongful cases so as to maintain judicial fairness. We will strive to promote the construction of an evidence-centered system of criminal charges. We will promote having defense counsel in the review for prosecution stage, and ensure lawyers' practice rights in accordance with the law. We will deepen the procuratorial mechanism of "remote stations + circuit inspections" to strengthen supervision of enforcement of criminal penalties and supervision activities. We will carry out a special supervision program on fraudulent civil litigation and will steadily promote supervision of illegal administrative acts. We will take the special legislation as an opportunity to strengthen work of public interest litigation. We will thoroughly implement the digital procuratorial strategy. We will deepen mechanisms for linking law enforcement supervision by the Political and Legal Affairs Commission of the Party Committee with the procuratorial organs' legal supervision , and explore mechanisms for linking legal supervision with rule of law supervision so as to make the legal supervision more powerful and effective.

Fifthly, we will ensure that the people can experience benefits of procuratorial work for the people. We will implement the principle of providing justice for the people, and launch the special campaign of "procuratorates safeguarding the people's livelihoods". We will further promote the rule of law in procuratorial xinfang, continue to strengthen governance of the sources of xinfang and the resolution of long-pending cases, increase support for prosecutions and judicial assistance, deepen procuratorial hearings, and create a procuratorial version of the "Fengqiao Experiences" for the New Era. We will resolutely strictly punish crimes endangering production safety, and strengthen judicial protection for people's livelihoods in areas such as food and drug safety, medical insurance, and protection of personal information. We will deepen cooperation with relevant departments to protect the legitimate rights and interests of minors, the elderly, women, persons with disabilities, and migrant workers in accordance with the law, and jointly protect rights and interests of workers in flexible employment and new forms of labor.

Sixthly, we will consistently improve capacity for legal supervision. We will fully implement Comrade Xi Jinping's important thought on the Party's self-revolution, persist in comprehensive and strict governance on the procuratorial team, and strengthen the integrated construction of political capacity, professional competences and professional ethics. We strengthen the procuratorate by strengthening the training of talents in short supply in intellectual property rights, finance and securities, and foreign-related with rule of law. We will deepen the implementation of the procuratorial reform plan, and strengthen restraint and supervision of the operation of procuratorial power. We will revise and improve the opinions on the implementation of the judicial responsibility system and the regulations on judicial accountability, implementing the punishment system for procurators, strengthening the management of procuratorial business, optimizing disclosure of procuratorial work, and further strengthening the fundamental construction of the primary procuratorates. We will deeply study and implement the newly revised Regulations on CPC Displinary Action and firmly carry out centralized disciplinary education so as to ensure our own competency through our own integrity and to build a strong procuratorial team.

Fellow Deputies, on our new journey in the New Era, we will unite more closely around the CPC Central Committee with Xi Jinping at the core, fully implementing the requirements of this meeting, and more consciously accept the oversight of the

NPC, democratic oversight and social oversight, and perform our legal supervision duties in accordance with the law so as to strive to create a new overall situation for the people's procuratorial undertakings, and make an even greater contribution to the comprehensive promotion of constructing a strong country and the great causes of national rejuvenation through Chinese modernization!

翻译：季美君　彭　玉　许慧君

校对：季美君　唐　哲（Jeremy Daum）

审校：张　清　刘静坤